short takes
making cooking simple
a cookbook by Jenny McClure

© Jenny McClure 2015
published by
McClure Publishers Ltd
Wellington, New Zealand, 2015
www.shorttakes.org

design by:
Shelley Masters

Jenny McClure is happy to hear from readers
mcclure@shorttakes.org

ISBN: 978-0-473-34198-5

This book is for Joe

Joe showed me how to see things differently.

How to use this book

This book is divided into five sections. Each section is colour-coded to make it easy to find.

Section one: grab a bite

These are quick and easy recipes. They're great when you're distracted, hungry and don't want to make a meal.

Section two: salads

Great for a light meal.

Section three: larger meals

These take a bit more time and attention. Use them when you want a full meal.

Section four: desserts

This section offers lots of different flavours, plus some old favorites.

Section five: odds and ends

These recipes are the 'home comfort' recipes.

This book has no fiddly measurements, fussy jargon or obscure ingredients.

The language is simple, the methods are easy.

It's designed for 'short takes'

Happy eating

contents

1 grab a bite

29 salads

43 larger meals

65 desserts

83 odds & ends

98 index

grab a bite

2 easy eggs on toast
4 tomatoes & balsamic
6 corn chip classic
8 asparagus with feta
10 salmon & toast
12 stuffed mushrooms
14 fruit toast
16 ploughman's lunch
18 artichoke toasts
20 Asian soup
22 avocado & pear
24 hot potato
26 buttered corn cob

easy eggs on toast

what you need:

 1 slice of bread

 1 egg

 1 tablespoon of milk

 1 teaspoon of butter, plus some for spreading

what you do:

1. **toast** then **butter** the bread

2. **break** the egg into a small bowl

3. **add** 1 tablespoon of milk and 1 teaspoon of butter

4. **beat** the mixture with a fork

5. **cook** in a microwave oven on **high** for one minute

6. **serve** on the toast.

serves 1

tomatoes & balsamic

what you need:

 2 slices of wholemeal bread
 cream cheese for spreading
 2 tomatoes
 1 teaspoon of sugar
 1 teaspoon balsamic vinegar

what you do:

1. **toast** the bread, then spread with cream cheese
2. **slice** the tomatoes and place them in a shallow dish
3. **cook** them in microwave oven on **high** for one minute
4. **sprinkle** with sugar and drizzle with balsamic vinegar
5. **set** microwave on **high** for another 20 seconds
6. **serve** on the toast - add salt and pepper to taste

serves 1

corn chip classic

what you need:

 3 handfuls of corn chips

 4 tablespoons of chilli beans

 ½ cup of grated cheddar cheese

 1 tablespoon of sour cream

what you do:

1. **lay** the corn chips in a shallow dish

2. **spread** the beans on top of the chips

3. **scatter** grated cheese on top of the beans

4. **cook** in a microwave oven on **high** for two minutes

5. **serve** topped with a tablespoon of sour cream

serves 1

asparagus with feta

what you need:

 1 slice of wholemeal bread

 cream cheese for spreading

 5 stalks of asparagus

 1 slice of feta (3cm/1" thick)

 juice from half a lemon

 pepper

what you do:

1. **toast** the bread then spread with cream cheese

2. **snap** the tough part off the end of each asparagus stalk

3. **place** asparagus stalks in a shallow dish

4. **cover** with water (you can cut them to fit the dish)

5. **cook** in a microwave oven on **high** for 3 minutes

6. **drain** the hot water off the asparagus (caution – hot dish)

7. **lay** the asparagus on the toast

8. **crumble** the feta and sprinkle it over the asparagus

9. **top** with squeezed lemon juice and fresh pepper

serves 1

salmon & toast

what you need:

 1 slice of toast

 cream cheese for spreading

 3 thin slices of smoked salmon

 a torn up salad leaf

 half a lemon

 fresh pepper

what you do:

1. **toast** the bread

2. **spread** the bread with cream cheese

3. **lay** the salmon slices on the toast

4. **garnish** with salad leaf

5. **top** with squeezed lemon juice and fresh pepper

serves 1

stuffed mushrooms

what you need:

 2 large flat mushrooms

 1 tablespoon of olive oil

 1 tablespoon of cream cheese

 ½ teaspoon of soy sauce

 1 tablespoon of cashew nuts

what you do:

1. **lay** the mushrooms on a flat dish, stalk side up
2. **drizzle** the olive oil over the two mushrooms
3. **top** each mushroom with half of the cream cheese
4. **drizzle** the soy sauce over the two mushrooms
5. **sprinkle** the cashews over the mushrooms
6. **cook** in a microwave oven on **high** for two minutes

serves 1

fruit toast

what you need:

 1 slice of toast

 cream cheese for spreading

 1 kiwi fruit

 1 banana

what you do:

1. **toast** the bread

2. **spread** the bread with cream cheese

3. **slice** the kiwi fruit onto the toast

4. **slice** and **pile** the banana on the toast

serves 1

ploughman's lunch

what you need:

 1 apple

 1 fresh bread roll

 butter for spreading

 Cheddar cheese

 2 ham slices

 several gherkins

 Ploughman's chutney

what you do:

1. **quarter** the apple
2. **arrange** the ingredients on a large plate
3. **cut** the bread roll in half and spread with butter
4. **fill** the roll with slices of cheese, ham and gherkins
5. **top** with chutney
6. **enjoy** with apple quarters

serves 1

artichoke toasts

what you need:

 1 small bread roll

 cream cheese for spreading

 2 artichoke hearts

 lemon zest (the grated skin of a lemon)

 black pepper

what you do:

1. **cut** the bread roll in half and **spread** with cream cheese

2. **cut** the artichoke hearts into quarters

3. **lay** the artichoke hearts on the cream cheese

4. **dust** with the grated lemon skin (lemon zest)

5. **top** with a few grinds of black pepper

serves 1

Asian soup

what you need:

 ½ tablespoon of hoisin sauce

 ½ tablespoon of oyster sauce

 ½ cup of water

 1 slice of tofu (3cm/1" thick)

 ½ cup of bean sprouts

 ½ cup of corn kernels

what you do:

1. **place** the hoisin sauce in a noodle bowl

2. **add** the oyster sauce and water

3. **stir** all together with a fork

4. **cut** the tofu into cubes

5. **add** the tofu, bean sprouts and corn kernels

6. **cook** in a microwave oven on **high** for 1 minute

serves 1

avocado & pear

what you need:

 2 slices of wholemeal bread

 cream cheese for spreading

 1 pear

 1 avocado

 half a lemon

 fresh pepper

what you do:

1. **toast** the bread and **spread** with cream cheese

2. **slice** the pear (discard the core)

3. **lay** the pear slices on the bread

4. **peel** and **slice** the avocado

5. **place** the avocado on top of the pear slices

6. **sprinkle** with lemon juice and fresh pepper

serves 1

hot potato

what you need:

- 1 large potato
- 1 teaspoon of butter
- ¼ cup of grated Cheddar cheese
- 1 tablespoon of sour cream
- paprika

what you do:

1. **poke** the potato three times with a knife
2. **place** a folded paper towel on a plate
3. **put** the potato on top of the folded paper towel
4. **cook** in a microwave oven on **high**.
   (5 mins for average sized potato, 7 mins for a big one)
5. **slice** down the middle of the potato to open it up
6. **spread** in the butter, cheese, sour cream
7. **dust** with paprika

serves 1

buttered corn cob

what you need:

 1 corn cob

 1 tablespoon of butter

 ¼ teaspoon of paprika

what you do:

1. **put** the whole corn cob, leaves and all, in the microwave
2. **cook** on **high** for 4 minutes
3. **take** the cob out of the microwave (use a cloth - it's hot)
4. **remove** the leaves from the cob
5. **smother** the corn with butter, dust with paprika
6. **eat** off the cob

serves 1

salads

30 Greek salad

32 melon salad

34 pear, walnut & blue cheese

36 couscous almond & date

38 lentil salad

40 salmon salad

Greek salad

what you need:

 2 tomatoes

 ¼ cucumber

 1 red onion

 1 capsicum

 1 slice of feta (3cm/1" thick)

 ¼ cup of olives

 5 teaspoons of olive oil

 1 teaspoon of lemon juice

 pepper

what you do:

1. **cut** the tomatoes into wedges, the cucumber into chunks
2. **cut** four thin slices off the onion and the capsicum
3. **cut** the slice of feta into chunks
4. **put** all the ingredients into a salad bowl
5. **add** ¼ cup of olives
6. **mix** the olive oil and lemon juice in a small dish
7. **pour** the olive oil and lemon juice mix over the salad
8. **top** with grinds of pepper

serves 2

melon salad

what you need:

- ½ a honeydew melon
- 1 avocado
- 2 kiwi fruit
- 1 tomato
- 2 thin slices prosciutto ham
- 5 teaspoons of olive oil
- ½ an orange for squeezing

what you do:

1. **peel** and **slice** the melon, avocado and kiwi fruit
2. **chop** the tomato into chunks
3. **tear** the ham slices into pieces
4. **place** the ingredients on a plate
5. **mix** the olive oil and 1 teaspoon of orange juice in a dish
6. **drizzle** the olive and orange juice mix over the salad
7. **top** with a grind of pepper

serves 2

pear, walnut & blue cheese

what you need:

 a handful of lettuce leaves

 1 pear

 1 tablespoon of walnuts

 1 slice of blue cheese (3cm/1" thick)

 5 teaspoons of olive oil

 1 lemon for squeezing

 pepper

what you do:

1. **slice** the pear into thin slices

2. **place** the lettuce, pear, walnuts, blue cheese on a plate

3. **toss** them all together

4. **mix** the olive oil and 1 teaspoon of lemon juice in a dish

5. **pour** the mix over the salad

6. **top** with some grinds of fresh pepper

serves 2

couscous, almond & date

what you need:

- ½ cup of water
- ½ cup of couscous
- 2 tablespoons of raisins
- 2 tablespoons of roast almonds
- 2 tablespoons of chopped dried apricots
- 1 tablespoon chopped dates
- 1 spring onion
- 1 orange

what you do:

1. **boil** a cup of water
2. **put** couscous in bowl, **add** the boiling water and let it stand for 3 minutes
3. **add** the raisins, almonds, apricots, dates
4. **chop** up the spring onion and **add** to the bowl
5. **mix** it all together
6. **squeeze** the juice of one orange over the salad

serves 2

lentil salad

what you need:

 2 sprigs of parsley

 1 can of lentils (410g/14.5oz)

 1 cup of raisins

 ⅓ cup capers

 ½ cup of walnut halves

 1 tablespoon of olive oil

 1 teaspoon of lemon juice

 1 tablespoon of cream cheese

what you do:

1. **cut** up the parsley
2. **empty** the can of lentils into a strainer
3. **wash** the lentils by running cold water over them
4. **place** the lentils in a salad bowl
5. **add** and **mix in** the raisins, capers, parsley, walnuts
6. **mix** the olive oil and 1 teaspoon of lemon juice in a dish
7. **stir** the mixture through the lentils
8. **top** with a tablespoon of cream cheese

serves 2

salmon salad

what you need:

- 2 oranges
- 1 thick slice of feta cheese (6cm/2" thick)
- 1 avocado
- 4 thin slices smoked salmon
- 1 cup of green salad leaves
- ¼ cup of sunflower seeds
- 1 tablespoon of olive oil
- 1 teaspoon of lemon juice

what you do:

1. **peel** and **segment** the oranges
2. **crumble** the feta slices
3. **peel** and **slice** the avocado
4. **tear** the salmon into pieces
5. **place** all the ingredients on a serving plate
6. **mix** the olive oil and lemon juice in a small dish
7. **drizzle** the olive oil and lemon juice mix over the salad

serves 2

larger meals

44 chicken & tomato

46 mixed bean meal

48 corn bake

50 chicken curry

52 creamy pasta

54 pasta, feta & tomato

56 pasta & artichokes

58 tomato topped flat bread

60 salmon topped flat bread

62 fish in foil

chicken & tomato

what you need:

 1 can of tomatoes (410g/14.4oz) - diced or crushed

1 tablespoon of sugar

1 tablespoon of balsamic vinegar

1½ tablespoons of soy sauce

 1 chicken breast boneless and skinless (200g/7oz approx)

 ½ cup of baby spinach leaves

 ½ cup of pitted black olives

 2 bread rolls

what you do:

1. **empty** the can of tomatoes into a pot

2. **add** the sugar, balsamic vinegar and soy sauce

3. **cut** the chicken into cubes and add to the pot

4. **heat** the mixture on the stovetop until it boils

5. let it **bubble gently** for fifteen minutes

6. **stir occasionally** while it is bubbling

7. **cut** up the spinach

8. **add** the spinach and olives just before serving

9. **serve** with a bread roll

serves 2

mixed bean meal
makes enough for a couple of meals

what you need:

- 1 can of white beans (400g/14oz)
- 1 can of red beans (400g/14oz)
- 1 can of chickpeas (400g/14oz)
- ½ cup of canned lentils (400g/14oz)
- ½ cup of couscous
- 1 tablespoon of ground cumin
- a handful of green salad leaves
- 1 tablespoon of cream cheese
- 1 can of baby beetroot (400g/14oz)

what you do:

1. **open** and **drain** the cans of beans, chickpeas and lentils
2. **put** one cup of water into a pot on the stovetop
3. **add** the beans, chickpeas and ½ cup of lentils
4. **heat** the mixture so it boils gently for 15 minutes
5. **add** ½ cup of couscous, 1 tablespoon of cumin
6. **add** salt and pepper to taste
7. **cook** the mixture for another 5 minutes
8. **stir** it to stop it sticking as it thickens
9. **chop** the salad leaves and use to garnish
10. **serve** with a baby beetroot and cream cheese

corn bake

what you need:

 a couple of thin slices of ham (50g/1.8oz)

 1 egg

 1 cup of corn kernels

 2 tablespoons of cream cheese

 ½ cup of grated cheddar cheese

 2 teaspoons of grated Parmesan cheese

 paprika

what you do:

1. **tear** the ham into bite-sized pieces

2. **break** the egg in a bowl and beat it with a fork

3. **mix** in the corn, cream cheese, grated cheese and ham

4. **sprinkle** Parmesan cheese on top and dust with paprika

5. **cover** the dish with plastic wrap

6. **cook** in a microwave oven on **high** for 3 minutes

serves 2

chicken curry

what you need:

 1 chicken breast (200g/7oz)

 1 tablespoon of olive oil

 1 tablespoon of green curry paste

 1 can of coconut cream (410g/14.5oz)

 1 tablespoon of fish sauce

 ½ cup of frozen beans

 1 naan bread

what you do:

1. **cut** the chicken into cubes

2. **heat** one tablespoon of oil in a pot on the stovetop

3. **add** one tablespoon of curry paste, fry for a few seconds

4. **add** the coconut cream, fish sauce and diced chicken

5. **keep** the **heat low** so it boils gently

6. **boil** until the chicken is cooked through (about 15 minutes)

7. **add** the green beans in the last few minutes of cooking

8. **serve** with naan bread

serves 2

creamy pasta

what you need:

 3 cups of water

 1 cup of dried penne pasta

 2 tablespoons of cream cheese

 ¼ teaspoon of grated lemon rind

 ¼ teaspoon of nutmeg

 ½ cup of baby spinach

 ¼ cup of roasted cashews

 grated Parmesan cheese

 pepper

what you do:

1. **put** three cups of water in a pot

2. **heat** the water on the stovetop until it boils

3. **add** one cup of dried pasta

4. **boil** gently for 9 minutes

5. **drain** the water from the pasta

6. **add** the cream cheese

7. **mix** the lemon rind into the mixture, **sprinkle** with nutmeg

8. **stir** so that the pasta is coated with mixture

9. **cut** up the spinach and mix in the spinach and nuts

10. **serve** with Parmesan cheese and fresh pepper

serves 2

pasta, feta & tomato

what you need:

 2 slices of feta

 ½ cup of baby spinach

 1 tablespoon of olives

 ¼ cup of sundried tomatoes

 1 tablespoon of balsamic vinegar

 1 cup of dried pasta shells

 grated Parmesan cheese

what you do:

1. **cut** feta slices into pieces

2. **slice** up the baby spinach

3. **put** the feta, olives and sundried tomatoes into a bowl

4. **add** the balsamic vinegar and baby spinach

5. **put** 2 cups of water in a pot, **bring to the boil** on the stove

6. **add** the pasta shells and cook for about 9 minutes

7. **drain** the hot water from the pasta shells

8. **mix** the pasta into the other ingredients

9. **sprinkle** with Parmesan cheese

serves 2

pasta & artichokes

what you need:

 ⅓ cup of frozen broad beans

 2 cups of water

 ½ cup of dried penne pasta

 ⅓ cup of bottled artichoke hearts

 ⅓ cup of sun dried tomatoes

 1 tablespoon of basil pesto

 grated Parmesan cheese

 fresh pepper

what you do:

1. **put** the frozen beans in a cup of hot water to defrost

2. **put** 2 cups of water in a pot, **bring to the boil** on the stovetop

3. **add** the pasta, **boil** gently for 9 minutes

4. **drain** the hot water from the pot

5. **cut** the artichoke hearts into quarters

6. **add** the artichokes to the drained pasta

7. **drain** the water off the beans

8. **add** the beans, sun dried tomatoes, pesto to the pot

9. **mix** together and serve

10. **top** with black pepper and grated Parmesan cheese

serves 2

tomato topped flat bread

what you need:

- 1 flat bread
- ½ cup of pizza sauce
- 2 slices of shaved ham
- 1 cup of grated mozzarella cheese
- ½ cup of olives

what you do:

1. **heat oven** to 180°C /350°F

2. **spread** the pizza sauce over the flat bread

3. **tear** the ham into bite sized pieces

4. **sprinkle** the ham, cheese and olives over the flat bread

5. **bake** for **15 minutes** in the oven

serves 2

salmon topped flat bread

what you need:

 1 flat bread

 ½ cup of sour cream

 4 thin slices of smoked salmon (100g/3.4oz)

 ½ cup of baby spinach

 6 thin slices of Brie cheese

what you do:

1. **heat oven** to 180°C/350°F

2. **spread** sour cream over the bread

3. **cut** the spinach into pieces

4. **spread** salmon, cheese and spinach over the flat bread

5. **bake** for **15 minutes** in the oven

serves 2

fish in foil

what you need:

 tin foil

 a piece of white fish (100g/3.4oz)

 ½ teaspoon of salt

 1 lemon

 ½ tablespoon of Thai Sweet Chili sauce

what you do:

1. **heat oven** to 95°C/200°F
2. **lay** a piece of foil on the bench (about 30cm/11" long)
3. **place** the fish in the middle of the foil
4. **sprinkle** half a teaspoon of salt on the fish
5. **squeeze** the juice from one half of the lemon over the fish
6. **spread** the Thai Sweet Chili sauce over the fish
7. **slice** the remaining lemon and lay the slices on the fish
8. **fold** the foil over the fish to form a neat parcel
9. **place** on baking tray and **bake** for **15 minutes** in the oven

serves 1

desserts

66 dried fruit salad & yoghurt

68 pears in wine

70 baked apple

72 bread pudding

74 cool berries

76 chia & guava

78 spiced strawberries

80 strawberries & melon

dried fruit salad & yoghurt

what you need:

 ½ cup of dried apricots

 ½ cup of dried prunes

 1 cinnamon quill

 1 cup of apple juice

 1 tablespoon of yoghurt

what you do:

1. **place** the dried fruit, cinnamon and apple juice in a bowl

2. **cook** in microwave oven at **50% power** for **8 minutes**

3. **leave** it to cool until the fruits are soft

4. **serve** with yoghurt.

serves 2

pears in wine

what you need:

 1 pear

 1 cup of water

 1 cup of wine

 1 tablespoon of sugar

 ½ teaspoon of nutmeg

 ½ teaspoon of cinnamon

 ice cream for serving

what you do:

1. **peel** a pear and place in a deep bowl

2. **add** the water, wine, sugar, nutmeg, cinnamon

3. **cook** in microwave oven on **high** for **6 minutes**

4. **remove** the pear from the liquid

5. **serve** with ice cream

serves 1

baked apple

what you need:

 1 apple

 1 tablespoon of sultanas

 2 teaspoons maple syrup

 plain yoghurt for serving

to remove the apple core use a small sharp knife and cut deeply around the core at the top and bottom of the apple, then push the core out

what you do:

1. **remove** the core of the apple
2. **score** a line around the middle of the apple to stop bursting
3. **stuff** the core hole with sultanas
4. **put** the apple on a plate
5. **pour** maple syrup into the stuffed core
6. **cook** in microwave oven on **high** for **3 minutes**
7. **poke** the apple with a knife to check cooking
8. **cook** for another minute if it is not cooked through
9. **cool** for a few minutes
10. **serve** with plain yoghurt

serves 1

bread pudding

what you need:

 1 tablespoon of butter

 1 egg

 1 tablespoon of sugar

 3 tablespoons of milk

 1 tablespoon of sultanas

 1 slice of white bread

 plain yoghurt for serving

what you do:

1. **chop** the butter into small pieces

2. **put** the butter pieces in a small bowl

3. **break** the egg into the bowl

4. **add** the sugar, milk and sultanas

5. **beat** the ingredients together with a fork

6. **tear** the bread into bite-sized pieces and put in the bowl

7. **stir** so the mixture covers the bread

8. **cover** with plastic wrap

9. **cook** in the microwave on **high** for **2½ minutes**

10. **serve** with plain yoghurt

serves 1

cool berries makes one large glass or two small ones

what you need:

 2 meringues

 1 cup of frozen berries

 ½ cup of plain yoghurt

what you do:

1. **break** the meringues into bite-sized pieces

2. **put** in a bowl the berries, yoghurt and meringue pieces

3. **stir** gently about three or four times

4. **spoon** the mixture into a glass

5. **put** in fridge until ready to serve

serves 1

chia & guava

what you need:

- 1 tablespoon of chia seeds
- 4 tablespoons of coconut cream
- ½ teaspoon of maple syrup
- 1 can of guavas (410g/14.5oz)

what you do:

1. **put** the chia seeds in a small bowl or cup

2. **add** the coconut cream and maple syrup

3. **stir** together until well mixed

4. **put** in the fridge for about 3 hours

5. **serve** with guavas

serves 1

spiced strawberries *serves 2*

what you need:

 1 tablespoon of brown sugar

 1 teaspoon of balsamic vinegar

 8 large strawberries

 plain ice cream for serving

what you do:

1. **put** the sugar and balsamic in a small bowl, **stir well**

2. **cut** the leaves off the strawberries

3. **put** the strawberries in a bowl

4. **drizzle** the mixture over the strawberries

5. **serve** with plain ice cream

serves 1

strawberries & melon

what you need:

 ½ teaspoon of lemon juice

 ½ teaspoon of honey

 8 strawberries

 slice of water melon (about 2.5cm/1" thick)

 ¼ teaspoon of lemon zest (grated lemon skin)

 cream cheese for serving

what you do:

1. **put** the lemon juice and honey in a small dish
2. **stir well**
3. **check** the taste, add more lemon juice if it's too sweet
4. **chop** the leaves off the strawberries
5. **chop** the melon into bite-size pieces
6. **put** the melon and strawberries into a bowl
7. **pour** the honey/lemon mixture over the fruit
8. **top** with grated lemon zest
9. **serve** with cream cheese

serves 2

odds & ends

84 chocolate bark

86 mango smoothie

88 berry smoothie

90 banana smoothie

92 nuts, fruits & cheese platter

94 porridge with nuts & maple

96 hot milk with nutmeg

chocolate bark

what you need:

 ½ cup cashew nuts

 ½ cup sultanas

 ¼ cup of pumpkin seeds

 ¼ cup sunflower seeds

 tinfoil

 butter

 a block of cooking chocolate (200g/7oz)

what you do:

1. **mix** the cashews, sultanas, pumpkin & sunflower seeds
2. **cover** a dinner plate with a piece of tinfoil
3. lightly **spread** a thin layer of butter over the tinfoil
4. **break** the chocolate block into pieces
5. **put** the chocolate in a microwave proof bowl
6. **cook** chocolate in microwave, **40% power** for **2 minutes**
7. **pour** the melted chocolate onto the tin foil
8. **scatter** the nut mix over the chocolate.
9. **push** the nuts into the chocolate using the back of a spoon
10. **put** in fridge for 1 hour then **cut** into pieces

several slices

mango smoothie

what you need:

 a blender

 1 cup of milk

 ½ cup of tinned mango

 1 tablespoon of yoghurt

what you do:

1. **put** all the ingredients in a blender

2. **whizz** together in the blender and serve

serves 1

berry smoothie

what you need:

   a blender

   1 cup of milk

   ½ cup of frozen berries

   1 tablespoon of yoghurt

what you do:

1. **put** all the ingredients in a blender

2. **whizz** together in the blender and serve

serves 1

banana smoothie

what you need:

 a blender

 1 cup of milk

 1 chopped banana

 1 tablespoon of yoghurt

what you do:

1. **put** all the ingredients in a blender

2. **whizz** together in the blender and serve

serves 1

nuts, fruits & cheese platter

what you need:

 a handful of almonds

 a handful of Brazil nuts

 a handful of dried apricots

 a handful of dried mango

 a favourite cheese

what you do:

1. **arrange** ingredients on a platter

2. **self serve**

serves 2

porridge with nuts & maple

what you need:

 ½ cup of porridge oats

 1 cup of milk

 1 tablespoon of sultanas

 1 tablespoon of walnuts

 1 tablespoon of maple syrup

 2 tablespoons of plain yoghurt

what you do:

1. **put** the oats, milk, sultanas and walnuts in a bowl

2. **cook** in a microwave oven on **high** for **2 minutes**

3. **top** with maple syrup, yoghurt and/or milk

serves 1

hot milk with nutmeg

what you need:

1 mug of milk

1 whole nutmeg

what you do:

1. **heat** the milk in a microwave oven on High for one minute

2. **grate** a quarter of the nutmeg into the hot milk

3. **stir twice**, sit back and enjoy

serves 1

A Apple 16, 70
Apricots – dried 66, 92
Artichoke hearts 18, 56
Asparagus 8
Avocado 22, 32, 40

B Banana 14, 90
Baby beets 46
Baby spinach 44, 52, 54, 60
Bean sprouts 20
Berries – frozen 74, 88
Brazil nuts 92
Bread – white 72
Broad beans 56

C Capsicum 30
Cheese – blue 34
Cheese – Brie 60
Cheese - Cheddar 6, 16, 24, 48
Cheese – Mozzarella 58
Chia seeds 76
Chili beans 6
Chicken 44, 50
Chick peas 46
Chocolate – cooking 84
Coconut cream 50, 76
Corn chips 6
Con cob 26
Corn kernels 20, 48
Couscous 36, 46
Cucumber 30

E Egg 2, 48, 72

F Fish – white 62
Flat bread 58, 60

G Guavas 76

H Ham 16, 32, 48

K Kiwi fruit 14, 32

L Lentils 38, 46

M Melon 32, 80
Meringues 74
Milk 72, 86, 88, 90, 94, 96
Mushrooms 12

N Nutmeg 96

O Oats 94
Oranges 40

P Pasta 52, 54, 56
Pear 22, 34, 68
Pizza sauce 58
Potato 24
Prunes – dried 66

R Raisins 36
Red beans 46

S Salad leaves 34, 40
Salmon - slices 40, 60
Strawberries 78, 80
Sun dried tomatoes 54
Sultanas 70, 72, 94

T Tomatoes 4, 30
Tomatoes – canned 44
Tofu 20

W Walnuts 34, 38, 94
White beans 46

Y Yoghurt 66, 70, 72, 74, 86, 88, 90, 94

index

www.ingramcontent.com/pod-product-compliance
Lightning Source LLC
Chambersburg PA
CBHW041157290426
44108CB00003B/99